MW00928134

Pigs
For Kids

Amazing Animal Books
For Young Readers

By
Rachel Smith

Mendon Cottage Books

Mendon Cottage Books
JD-Biz Corp Publishing

All Rights Reserved.

No part of this publication may be reproduced in any form or by any means, including scanning, photocopying, or otherwise without prior written permission from JD-Biz Corp

Copyright © 2015. All Images Licensed by Fotolia and 123RF.

Read More Amazing Animal Books

Purchase at Amazon.com

Table of Contents

Introduction

Pigs have long been a part of human life. The ancient Israelites considered them unclean animals, and would not eat them; however, many, many cultures consider them a great source of food.

The pig is present in the Chinese zodiac, a way of keeping track of years by assigning twelve animals, one to each year. It's also said to predict traits and such about people born in those years. It's the twelfth sign, because, according to legend, the pig showed up last to the great meeting where the animals were assigned to a system.

The pig has long been a sign of gluttony, especially in Western culture. In the book Animal Farm, they greedily consume the best of the food, and do almost none of the work.

Pigs are considered dirty, but the fact is, they tend to be very clean animals. They do consume a lot of food, but not all pigs are fat; it's mostly domesticated (bred to serve humans) pigs that are as obese-looking as you see in the modern day.

They are very interesting creatures.

What is a pig?

Pigs are members of the genus Sus. Most people are familiar with pink piggies on farms, but those are only the domesticated kind. Domesticated means that humans have bred them over many years to be used for human survival. Humans have long kept pigs.

A row of young domesticated pigs.

A male pig is called a boar, a female a sow, and the babies are called piglets.

The domesticated pig is descended from the wild boar, a pig that is still around in Europe and Asia. But there are vast differences between nowadays' pink pig and the hairy, tusked wild boar.

The domesticated pig, in comparison to the wild boar, has less hair, or less noticeable hair. It also has been domesticated for over 5,000 years, meaning that there's been a lot of time for humans to shape pigs the way they want them to be through breeding. For instance, many pigs get fatter than wild boars, or have tastier meat.

But there are a few things most pigs have in common.

One is that they are all omnivores. In the pig's case, this means they will eat anything edible. This can include other animals and even humans, on rare occasions. Pigs will live well in any area or setting that has a lot of food. If they are wild pigs, they will have their population fluctuating as they get to be too big a group for their habitat, and then as they get smaller again.

Pigs are native to Europe, Asia, and Africa; however, they live throughout the world. The problem for a lot of places is that these pigs get released as either game or on accident, so that the natural balance is thrown out of whack. Pigs like these are often called feral pigs.

Pigs have large heads and stout bodies; they heads have long snouts, and they have a special nose bone that helps support the length. They also have forty-four teeth, and in males, the canines (the pointy teeth-humans have them too!) turn into tusks that they can fight with. Their back teeth are made for grinding, just like human molars.

The snout has a disk of cartilage (the bendy stuff that makes up your ears and nose) at the end. This is why pigs' noses are rounded. It's an incredibly sensitive organ, and pigs often use it to dig in the dirt for food.

Some pigs, particularly domestic or captive pigs, have trouble when they have babies. The mamas might accidently crush their babies, or sometimes, if they're really stressed out, they'll hurt their babies on purpose. This is why a lot of farmers separate the baby pigs from their mamas as soon as possible.

Piglets, when they are born, get their tails clipped and their potential tusks clipped. This is why we never see boars with tusks with domestic pigs. The main reason for this is so that the piglets don't hurt each other.

There are around a billion pigs throughout the world at this moment. This makes them one of the largest populations of large mammals throughout the world.

Pigs also have small lungs in comparison to their bodies, so they are more likely to be hurt by things like bronchitis. Pigs can also catch human influenza.

They are also fairly aggressive; if they're trying to protect themselves or their piglets, they may hurt humans. Some people say that pigs resent being domesticated, and they are pretty intelligent animals, so there is probably some truth to it.

What kinds of pigs are there?

There are many types of pigs. The main known one is the domestic pig, but there are other, wild pigs throughout the world. There are also animals that don't belong to the genus Sus but are considered pigs or pig-related.

A Bornean bearded pig.

First, there are the true pigs. These included domesticated pigs, wild pigs, bearded pigs and warty pigs. Wild pigs are domesticated pigs that somehow ended up back in the wild. They could have escaped, been released to be hunted, or other reasons.

Bearded pigs are more common to Asia, and are very hairy; many kinds have fluffs of hair, as shown in the picture. Warty pigs have, you guessed it, warts all over their faces.

There are quite a few kinds of both bearded and warty pigs. Besides the wild boar, there really aren't a lot of pigs immediately related to the domestic pig.

The domestic pig is considered different enough from the wild boar by many to be a different species. Other experts don't believe that, saying that it hasn't evolved enough to be a separate species.

Then, there are the related pigs: the babirusa, the warthog, red river hogs, peccaries, and more. Most are considered hogs of a sort, even if they aren't as closely related to pigs.

Thanks to humans, pigs of many kinds can be found throughout the world, even on deserted islands and places like Australia and New Zealand. The pigs in places such as North and South America have caused a lot of trouble for the local wildlife, since they throw things out of balance.

Where did pigs come from?

Pigs evolved from early ancestors; the ones we know the most about are from China. Many prehistoric pig remains have been found there.

So, the likelihood is that the pigs originated near or in what is now China. The world was very different back then, however, and Chinese people didn't exist yet (at least not as a culture). Many even suspect that humans as we know them didn't exist yet.

Humans tamed pigs long after these pigs went into extinction.

However, it still cool to know that the pig has been around for a very long time, even if they used to be different.

The history of pigs and humans

Pigs have been domesticated from at least 5,000 years ago. Humans have relied on pigs quite a bit throughout history, and they have proven to be very useful to humans.

A farmer on a pig farm.

Pigs have long been a part of the human diet. Pork, which includes ham and bacon, accounts for a big chunk of the world's meat consumption. Pigs have never been used for anything other than food, leather, and their bristle; their bristles, which are basically hairs, are used in some brushes.

Humans tamed pigs to an extent thousands of years ago. There are two ways that pigs are raised for food nowadays: though a confined (small and shut) space, where they are fed slop, or through letting them forage with someone watching, called a swineherd. Pigs are often called swine, and a swineherd is the traditional way of raising pigs.

In commercialized pig farming, which means a company or a very large farm is doing the farming, they often have small spaces, and are fed specially prepared diets so that they grow the way that the farmers want them to grow.

Pigs are also kept as pets. This is most common with pot-bellied pigs, who, as the name suggest, have a rounded pot belly. The problem for most people is that while baby pigs are small and cute, a pig is a huge commitment. They live fairly long, and eat a lot. When a pot-bellied pig is full grown, it may prove too much for the owners to handle.

It's unfortunately often that pet pigs are gotten rid of once they become adults because the owners don't think they're cute anymore.

Pigs are also used to hunt for truffles in Europe. Truffles are a sort of fungus that is very expensive; in fact, it's a part of the most expensive burger in the world. Pigs are excellent at finding them due to their great sense of smell.

Babirusas (also known as pig-deer)

A babirusa, as stated above, is also called a pig-deer. This is because of its long legs, and its relation to pigs.

A Babirusa in Indonesia.

Babirusas are considered a kind of pig. It is part of the pig family Suidae, though it doesn't belong to the genus Sus and therefore is not what we consider a traditional pig. They have curled tusks, which they must wear down, or else they might grow long enough to hurt the babirusa.

They are interestingly different from many pigs, in that the tusks grow up and backwards, pointing towards its own face.

Babirusas live in Sulawesi, the Sula Islands, and Buru, as a few of its habitats. Those places are in Indonesia, which is a country which is a large group of islands. Strangely, there's an island in between the places that the babirusa lives, but none of them live there. Some people suggest that it was moved by people, and that's why it doesn't occur on that island.

Babirusas have intestinal tracts that are very similar to domestic pigs. Different types have different fur, from brown to golden to even almost bald.

This kind of pig lives in two different ways: males live alone, and don't socialize with any other babirusas except for mating. Females and piglets live together in small groups, and the females look out for the piglets.

Males fight each other with their tusks; the lower ones they use for defense, and the upper for attack.

Pot-belled pigs

Pot-bellied pigs are cute pigs that come from Vietnam. They've recently gained a liking as a pet for people in places like America, but they've always been used for food in Vietnam.

A black pot-bellied pig.

They are smaller than domestic European or American pigs, and this is one reason they are considered cute. Also, babies tend to be absolutely adorable.

Pot-bellied pigs weren't bred in the same way in Vietnam as the domestic pigs in America and Europe were. They are very closely related to the wild boar and the domestic pig, but their genetics are more varied. This is because Vietnamese farmers didn't breed the pigs for a specific standard throughout all of Vietnam. Instead, every region has different pot-bellied pigs.

This is because Vietnam did not reach quite the level in breeding that many European and American countries. This is partly due to colonialism; Vietnam was taken over during about the 19th century by France, and made part of a group called French Indochina. French Indochina was not developed by the French to be an advanced country; instead, it was used for its resources.

The chief characteristic of pot-bellied pigs are the pot bellies. It curves towards the ground, much like a big gut on a human, if they were standing on all fours.

This type of pig still lives in the wild in Vietnam, and some kinds of sturdier pigs have been introduced to strengthen the pig population. They mostly live in the mountains and parts of Thailand nowadays.

The problem for pot-bellied pigs, as mentioned before, is that they are often abandoned once they reach adulthood. Most people don't realize just how big that cute little piglet will get, and they aren't prepared to take care of a 100-300 pound animal. Some also are forced to give them up because they're too big for the local laws.

You should always research pets thoroughly before you get one; too many people get the cute baby and release the defenseless adult into the wild.

Red river hogs

Red river hogs are sometimes called bush pigs. They live in parts of Africa, and are very distinctive by their reddish colored fur.

A red river hog.

This type of pig lives in the rainforest, near swamps and rivers. It's rare to catch them outside of that environment. Unlike some kinds of pig, it is native to all its habitats, as no one has exported the red river hog.

Red river hogs are not so popular among plantation owners. This is because, since the animal is an omnivore, it eats just about anything, and anything includes plantation crops. However, it does far more damage by rooting around with its nose looking for things like insects and roots.

Their food can include berries, insects, roots, and even dead animals, though they don't tend to hunt for other animals.

Red river hogs live in groups. Usually, there is one boar, and then a number of sows, who each have three to six piglets. They are social animals, and it would be very unusual to find one living on its own. The boar will always be aggressively defensive of its herd.

They are around the same weight as pot-bellied pigs.

They are also nocturnal, and they come out in groups to look for food. Also, they have a very pretty sort of call pattern, which is said to sound like a part of a classical music symphony.

Wild Boars

Wild boars are the pigs that we know and love (and sometimes fear). It is an incredibly widespread animal, from its home in Eurasia (where it is sometimes called a Eurasian pig or wild swine) to almost every place on earth.

A group of baby wild boars.

As has already been mentioned, the wild boar is where the domestic pig comes from. It's a big, sturdy animal, with thick fur and thin, small legs.

They no longer live in the United Kingdom, having died out before the English even had the words to specify between domestic pigs and the wild boar.

Wild boars come in four kinds, not even mentioning subspecies:

Western, which includes several kinds and has a high skull, for the most part. They also have thick underwool, since they belong to the European part of the world, which can get very cold.

Indian, which includes two kinds. These kinds have almost no underwool, and they have bands on their snouts.

Eastern, which have a whitish streak and no mane.

And Indonesian, which has almost no fur, underwool, or mane. It is one kind in this group, so there are no ways to compare it.

Wild boars have a female-dominated society, with a matriarch (female mother-like leader) ruling over a sounder, which is a group of barren (unable to have more babies) sows and young mother sows. Males only stay until a certain age; sometimes very young males may stay together in a group, when they're not quite adults yet, but the adult males and elderly males live alone.

Piglets whose mothers die in these groups will always be adopted by other mothers.

Wild boars are hunted by several kinds of animals, from lynx to brown bears. Its most common predator is the gray wolf, however, which seems to be in most of its natural habitat. The gray wolf seems to make a habit of hunting wild boars even when there is other prey available.

Many cultures consider the boar a symbol of bravery and being tough.

Feral Pigs

Feral pigs are domesticated pigs that somehow escaped domestication and live in the wild. They are a growing problem in many places.

Some captured feral pigs.

There are a lot of wild pigs in the Scottish highlands, for example. This is a problem because they ruin crops and overrun other animals. However, the problem in Scotland is not as bad as in places like North America, South America, Australia, and New Zealand.

Australia has quite the history with foreign animals being introduced to its isolated ecosystems. The biggest problem they have right now, and have had for a while, was with rabbits that a man set free to hunt. Now, the rabbit is hated in Australia for its unopposed destruction of habitats and crops.

Feral pigs are a big problem too. The big issue with animals being released in an environment that is not their own is that they overrun local populations. They don't have natural predators, so nothing stops them from growing way too big and possibly even causing the extinction of other, native creatures. This isn't their fault, of course; it's the humans who put them there's fault.

They also run across the United States, typically called 'wild hogs'. Wild boars are not native to the United States either, so escaped wild boars and feral pigs are often lumped together.

One of the reasons pigs were released (even Christopher Columbus did so) was that the explorers wanted to make sure there would be plenty of food for future explorers and colonists coming through. This was done hundreds of years ago, and many explorers thought it was a very good idea to release non-native animals into new settings.

We'll never know the full extent of the damage they did by doing so.

Peccaries

A peccary is also called a javelina or skunk pig. This is because of their patterning.

A collared peccary nursing its piglets.

Peccaries are what are called New World Pigs; they are not related to the wild boar or any pig from the Old World, or Asia, Europe, or Africa.

They are very similar to pigs, with similar noses and general looks. They live in groups of about eight or fifteen peccaries. It has three chambers in its stomach, and its stomach is more complicated than an old world pig's. There are three or four types of peccaries.

This type of pig lives in South America. It is (though not as much as it used to be) a food source for many of the peoples of that area.

Warthogs

Warthogs are called warthogs because of four wart-like parts of its face. They are a member of the pig family, and live in Africa.

A warthog in the water.

Warthogs tend to weigh a little more than pot-bellied pigs. They also tend to be larger. This type of pig is called the "Pig of the Plains" in Afrikaans. This is because its typical environment is on the Savannah.

The Savannah is a place that has mostly grasses, and not very many trees. It is a large part of Africa, but since Africa is a continent and not a country, the terrain (ground and plants) is very different in many different parts.

Like the wild boar, the warthog lives in groups called sounders. This consists of females and their young, just like wild boars, and the males tend to be solitary. However, the difference is that warthogs are less protective of territory and instead live a 'home range', or a wide area that they don't mind much if other animals enter.

They only breed seasonally; this is because certain seasons are better for piglets to be born in. Adult males only interact with females around this time.

Conclusion

Pigs are cute, funny, and interesting creatures. They are some of the most widespread on Earth, and they will probably always inhabit it.

Every kind of pig has its own charms and interesting facts. Hopefully, you have enjoyed this book and learned a lot about pigs.

But always remember: pigs are big pets, and they need a lot of care!

Author Bio

Rachel Smith is a young author who enjoys animals. Once, she had a rabbit who was very nervous, and chewed through her leash and tried to escape. She's also had several pet mice, who were the funniest little animals to watch. She lives in Ohio with her family and writes in her spare time.

Our books are available at
1. Amazon.com

2. Barnes and Noble

3. Itunes

4. Kobo

5. Smashwords

6. Google Play Books

Publisher

JD-Biz Corp

P O Box 374

Mendon, Utah 84325

http://www.jd-biz.com/

Mendon Cottage Books

P O Box 374, Mendon Utah 84325

82226722R00022

Made in the USA
Middletown, DE
01 August 2018